THE   OK

SO YOU THINK YOU KNOW

DAVID BECKHAM?

THE UNOFFICIAL QUIZ BOOK

SO YOU THINK YOU KNOW

DAVID BECKHAM?

CLIVE GIFFORD

Hodder
Children's
Books

a division of Hodder Headline Limited

© Copyright Hodder Children's Books 2003

Published in Great Britain in 2003
by Hodder Children's Books

Editor: Katie Sergeant
Design by Fiona Webb
Cover design: Hodder Children's Books

10 9 8 7 6 5 4 3 2

ISBN: 0340877650

Printed by Bookmarque Ltd, Croydon, Surrey

The paper and board used in this paperback by Hodder Children's Books are natural recyclable products made from wood grown in sustainable forests. The manufacturing processes conform to the environmental regulations of the country of origin.

Hodder Children's Books
a division of Hodder Headline Limited
338 Euston Road
London NW1 3BH

CONTENTS

INTRODUCTION

So you think you know all about the footballer, fashion icon and world-famous celebrity, David Beckham? You think you've got all the knowledge you need to tackle questions on his early career right the way through to the season after the 2002 World Cup? Well, make sure you kick-off and get in good scoring form with the warm ups section first as there is a long season of quizzes ahead. There are questions on David's Manchester United and England career, his early progress through the ranks, his family, friends and team-mates. Some you will know instantly. Others you might find as tough as the hard-tackling defenders David has faced in his career.

The questions are divided into three levels of difficulty, shown by a football rating at the top of each page – one football ⚽ for easy questions, two footballs ⚽⚽ for medium and three ⚽⚽⚽ for hard questions.

Hope you enjoy the challenge and don't forget to team up with a friend to have a go at our quiz version of a penalty shootout.

WARM UPS

1. Which country does David play football for?

2. Is he married, single or divorced?

3. Which club does he play for?

4. David played in all the games for England in Euro 96: true or false?

5. What number shirt does David Beckham wear at Manchester United?

6. What nationality is David's mother?

7. What band did Victoria sing in when she met David?

8. David hopes to become a pop singer after retiring from football: true or false?

9 The father of one of David's closest friends is called Neville Neville: true or false?

10 Does David have any children: yes or no?

11 What is the first name of David's wife?

12 What was David's wife's nickname in the band she used to sing in?

13 David missed one of the penalties in the Euro 96 shootout: true or false?

14 Against which team was he sent off in the 1998 World Cup?

15 David scored his first World Cup finals goal in 1998 or 2002?

16 Which pair of brothers has David played football with for many years at Manchester United?

17 What number is always part of the registration of any car David buys?

18　David sat in the front row for five nights of the Spice Girls' last tour: true or false?

19　Was 'Forever' the title of the Spice Girls' first, second or third album?

20　David's first child was named after a part of New York, a part of Manchester or a part of France?

21　Which Welsh team-mate of David's often plays on the left wing?

22　David attracted newspaper stories for wearing a sarong, a bra or a top hat to a party?

23　Who took David to see his first Manchester United game?

24　The Beckhamdaloo is a genuine curry dish served at an Indian restaurant in Wales: true or false?

25　Which team, one of Manchester United's great rivals, plays at Highbury?

Unjumble these letters to come up with the names of some of David's Manchester United team-mates. **(See answers on p149.)**

```
R N W J A N O T L O B P
H K O K H U J I P X E J
C H K T U W V F J X V L
I C B O L E C X O S E A
W E T I R R D Q B I R N
S Y L P R R A L P R T E
P N O T P M A H T U O S
I O M M S C I C C S N R
L D N A K A H N M L I A
Y A W B H E C N G J M C
W Q U F L L A W I H X Q
F R Y S F H U S E F A K
N D E R B Y O F F N X M
M A D N A L R E D N U S
```

Arsenal	Bolton	Liverpool
Charlton	Derby	Newcastle
Chelsea	Everton	Southampton
Birmingham	Fulham	Sunderland
Blackburn	Ipswich	

(See answers on p150.)

1   Which young striker from Everton did David praise at the start of 2003?

2   How many Premiership teams has David Beckham played for?

3   David loves fast cars and owns a Porsche, a Mercedes and an Aston Martin: true or false?

4   David has never captained England: true or false?

5   Is David displayed as a waxwork at Madame Tussauds?

6   What is the first name of David's eldest son?

7   To which country did he travel to play in the 2002 World Cup?

8   Who is David's manager at Manchester United?

9   Was David born in London, Manchester, Leeds or Birmingham?

10 David has a brother who plays in goal for Leyton Orient: true or false?

11 Was David on the BBC list of the 100 Greatest Britons?

12 According to Gary Neville, which Manchester United player signs more autographs than any other at the club?

13 Who, as of Autumn 2002, was Manchester United's most expensive signing?

14 David's famous mohican haircut cost £900 at a top hair salon: true or false?

15 Which high street store stocked Beckham's first clothing range?

16 Which team knocked England out of the 2002 World Cup?

17 The University of Staffordshire has a course about David Beckham: true or false?

18 What sort of king and queen-styled furniture did Victoria and David have as a feature at their wedding?

19 What part of the body did David injure shortly before the 2002 World Cup?

20 The first time he was to play for England, David turned up with an autograph book to collect signatures: true or false?

21 In what year was David's clothing range for boys launched in Britain?

22 Was Beckham rejected from England Schoolboys because he was considered too rude, too small or too slow?

23 In the *David Beckham Soccer* computer game, users can even change his hairstyle: true or false?

24 The Manchester derby match is played between which two clubs?

25 David's first child was a son or daughter?

1 Which team did England have to play in a two game play-off to enter the 2000 European Championships?

2 Does Beckham play in midfield, attack or defence?

3 What is the first name of David's mate and Phil Neville's brother?

4 Was David signed to Manchester United for free, for one million or 20 million pounds?

5 David has had a full-size snooker table put into his new mansion: true or false?

6 In the summer of 2001, David shaved off half an eyebrow, both his eyebrows or his goatee beard?

7 David met which famous politician at No. 10 Downing Street in May 2002?

8 David and Victoria's mansion in Hertfordshire has an indoor pool, an outdoor pool or no swimming pool?

9   David sang a little bit of backing vocals on a single of Victoria's: true or false?

10   From which country does David's England manager, Sven-Goran Eriksson, come from?

11   Two ex-team-mates of David's now play as strikers for Blackburn. Name one of them.

12   R&B star, Usher, is one of David's musical heroes: true or false?

13   In 1996, which English competition did Manchester United win apart from the league?

14   'The Beckham', eggs and fries, is a meal served at a well-known fast food restaurant: true or false?

15   Does David's home club ground hold more than 40,000, 50,000 or 60,000 spectators?

16   In the *David Beckham Soccer* computer game, users can place

David in the pop charts singing a
Spice Girls' song: true or false?

17 David played at Highfield Road in
1995. What opposition team,
beginning with the letter C, play
there?

18 How many goals did David score in
the 4-0 defeat of Spurs in March
2002?

19 Does David never, rarely or almost
always sign autographs?

20 David turned up to a Nottinghamshire
golf club hoping to play in a pair of
flip-flops: true or false?

21 In the 1999 Champions League final,
who took the corners from which
Manchester United scored twice?

22 Does he prefer to be the first, second
or last player out of the changing
room before a game?

23 David's ex-team-mate, Jaap Stam,
comes from which country?

24   David hopes to become a referee when he retires from football: true or false?

25   Both of Manchester United's 1999 Champions League final goals were scored by substitutes: true or false?

MATCH FIT 1

Match the grounds where David has played with the teams who play there.
(See answers on p146.)

St James Park	Manchester City
White Hart Lane	Southampton
Riverside	Bolton Wanderers
The Valley	Sunderland
Goodison Park	Birmingham City
St Andrews	Charlton Athletic
The Stadium of Light	Newcastle United
The Reebok Stadium	Middlesbrough
St Mary's Stadium	Everton
Maine Road	Tottenham Hotspur

FIRST HALF

1. Did David score a total of 8, 16 or 31 goals in the 2001-2002 season?

2. Callaghan Stoneware once manufactured Posh and Becks gnomes for sale: true or false?

3. What is Victoria's middle name: Jasmine, Caroline or Geri?

4. David swapped shirts at the end of a World Cup game with Carlos Valderrama. Which country was he playing against?

5. On BBC Radio One, David said that his biggest hero was an opera singer, a boxer, a politician or a basketball player?

6. Which striker scored the winner against Poland in 1996 from one of David's crosses?

7   Was the attendance at David's first
    England game: 9,000, 39,000,
    59,000 or 79,000?

8   Was the England team base for
    the 1998 World Cup at Malaga,
    La Manga or Ibiza?

9   At which football ground in the
    Midlands of England did David first
    captain England in a home game?

10 David's 57 yard strike against
    Wimbledon is a record for the
    longest distance goal ever in the
    Premiership: true or false?

11 In what continent is Moldova, the
    country that David faced in his first
    game for England?

12 Which Chelsea player scored the
    winning goal in David's first match
    against Italy?

13 David kept in touch with Preston
    North End after his short loan spell
    there: true or false?

14 How many English teams started the first group stage of the Champions League in 2002 apart from Manchester United?

15 Victoria's wedding dress has been on display in which London museum?

16 David came on as a substitute in a 1998 World Cup game played at Toulouse. Against which side did he play?

17 Apart from his dad, which member of his family joined in David's early football practice sessions?

18 Which team-mate of David's came to Manchester United from the Argentinean team, Independiente?

19 Did David's parents have their honeymoon in Barbados, Bognor Regis or Belgium?

20 What is the name of the ground, beginning with D, at which Preston North End play?

21 How old was David when he first scored from the halfway line: 13, 15, 16 or 18?

22 Which football manager won a lifetime achievement award at the same event in which David won BBC Sports Personality of the Year?

23 The Spice Girls' debut single was released first in which country?

24 What is Brooklyn Beckham's middle name?

25 David once dated Miss UK, Anna Bartley: true or false?

⚽ ⚽ **FIRST HALF 2** ⚽ ⚽

1 About which Frenchman did David once say: "He is the best I've ever played with"?

2 David scored a fierce shot in October 1996 against Liverpool, QPR or Bristol City?

3 David often practises free kicks in his bare feet: true or false?

4 What sort of flower does David regularly send Victoria when they are apart?

5 David was offered £100,000 to pose nude in a magazine: true or false?

6 David once whisked Victoria on a surprise visit to which Italian city famous for its canals?

7 Which Irish midfielder has been the long-serving captain at Manchester United?

8 By the end of October 2002, how many times had David been sent off whilst playing for Manchester United?

9 In what film did look-alikes play the parts of David and Victoria at an airport?

10 What was the name of the FIFA competition Manchester United attended in January 2000?

11 David attended a party given by Jade Jagger, Drew Barrymore or Britney Spears to launch some new jewellery?

12 Which one of the following Manchester United players didn't wear the no. 7 shirt: George Best, David Beckham, Sir Bobby Charlton or Bryan Robson?

13 Which player arrived for his transfer in 2001 wearing a no. 7 Manchester United shirt?

14 David and Victoria were married by the Bishop of Kerry, The Bishop of Cork or the Bishop of Dublin?

15 Who did England play in their first game of the 1998 World Cup?

16 Which British television channel did the Spice Girls help to launch?

17 The final of the Bobby Charlton Soccer Skills Tournament was held in which British city?

18 David's first goal for his club in the 2002-2003 season was against Chelsea, Arsenal, West Ham or Charlton?

19 Before 2002, what year last saw Manchester United lose to Manchester City: 1946, 1989 or 1995?

20 Who dropped David for the opening World Cup match in the 1998 finals?

21 David's mother is Welsh: true or false?

22 Against which South American team was his first international goal for England?

23 Has David ever served as vice-captain of the England team?

24 What number shirt did David have before switching to his current number 7?

25 A former striker team-mate of David's now plays for Spurs. Can you name him?

PENALTY SHOOTOUT 1

Play against a friend, taking turns to read out and answer the questions. If the scores are level after five questions each, whoever gets closest to the sudden death question is the winner.

(See answers on p145.)

Penalty Shootout 1

A1 David never played in midfield for England with Paul Gascoigne: true or false?

B1 David never played in midfield for England with Bryan Robson: true or false?

A2 David missed the 2002 Manchester derby. At what ground was the game played?

B2 What was the score of the 2002 Manchester derby match?

A3 Brian McClair, a former team-mate of David's, had the nickname: "Chubby", "Chippy" or "Choccy"?

B3 David's friend, Phil Neville, scored his first goal for Manchester United after 40, 50, 70 or 90 appearances?

A4 David and Victoria paid for a 17 year-old-girl to have artificial legs, artificial arms or a new heart?

B4 Roger Narbett worked as a team chef, team physio or team boot cleaner for the England 2002 World Cup squad?

A5 Which team, one of Manchester United's great rivals, plays at Elland Road?

B5 Which team, one of Manchester United's great rivals, plays at Anfield?

Sudden Death Question

How many points did David score in the Bobby Charlton Soccer Skills Tournament?

1   David's third lodgings in Manchester as a teenager were two kilometres, ten kilometres or 100 metres from Manchester United's training ground?

2   In what position did Manchester United finish the Premiership 2001-2002 season?

3   David was part of the England team that won the 1997 Le Tournoi competition: true or false?

4   What football show does David say he video tapes every weekend?

5   In August 2002, David scored one of the four, five or six goals Manchester United put past Zalaegerszegi TE?

6   What colour were David and Victoria's matching wedding outfits?

7   What was the nickname given to the crop of brilliant youngsters at Manchester United in the 1950s?

8   What went wrong at David's first
    Wembley appearance: his name was
    spelt wrongly on his shirt, he was
    sent off, he was injured by a thrown
    water bottle?

9   Between the 1992-1993 and the
    2001-2002 season, how many times
    did Manchester United win the
    Premiership title?

10 What is tattooed on David's back
    above the name of his son?

11 Which German team knocked
    Manchester United out of European
    competition in the 1996-1997
    season?

12 Who told David face-to-face that he
    had been selected to make his debut
    for England: Glenn Hoddle, David's
    dad, Paul Ince or Sir Alex Ferguson?

13 Manchester United toured South-east
    Asia, South America or South Africa
    before the start of the 2001-2002
    season?

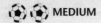

14 Which famous US boxer did David and Victoria watch in action in Manchester in 2000?

15 Who was David's second England game against: Spain, Poland or Portugal?

16 Which Manchester United player used to pretend he was Victoria as a joke on David?

17 Which club is David's dad a lifelong supporter of?

18 Before the Bayer Leverkusen game in November 2002, had David scored 27, 37, 47 or 57 league goals for Manchester United?

19 On 22 February 1997, Beckham scored the equalising goal against which London club?

20 In February 1997, David scored a goal with a shot that was measured at 57.9 mph, 77.9 mph or 97.9 mph?

21 David pulled out of the 2002 friendly match with Portugal with an injury to his calf, hip, toe or shoulder?

22 During the 2002 World Cup, whose name translated into Japanese, was stitched into his football boots?

23 David has scored more away goals than home goals in most seasons for Manchester United: true or false?

24 Who was the Manchester United manager before Sir Alex Ferguson?

25 Which team knocked England out of the 1998 World Cup?

FIRST HALF 4

1 Against which African nation did David sit on the bench and watch Paul Gascoigne and Jamie Redknapp stretchered off?

2 Which team did David make his England debut against?

3   Were Manchester United top, second
    or fourth seeds for the second group
    stage of the Champions League
    2002-2003?

4   When service station staff returned
    David's lost wallet, did David ring
    them personally, send them gifts,
    give them free tickets to Old Trafford
    or all of those things?

5   In 2000, did David win, come second
    or did not feature in the European
    Footballer of the Year competition?

6   What national side did David and
    England face in their first Le Tournoi
    game in 1997?

7   Which World Cup-winning team did
    England beat in their country in
    1997?

8   David admits to getting more
    nervous about playing golf, playing
    computer games or playing football
    in front of others?

9 David jumped on to the back of the scorer of the FA Cup final winning goal in 1996 in celebration. Who was the goal scorer?

10 For Rage Computer Games, he chose his Manchester United dream team. Who did he select for the number seven shirt?

11 Victoria performed her first solo single at the 2000 Party in the Park in front of which member of the royal family?

12 Who managed the England football team at the 2002 World Cup?

13 Chase Lane Park is where David first met Victoria, where he played his first proper matches or where he first met Gary Neville?

14 Which was the only English team not to make it into the second group stage of the 2002-2003 Champions League?

15 Which team's football kit did David receive as a present every Christmas?

16 The Manchester United side of the mid-1990s, which included David, was nicknamed: "The Little Red Devils", "Fergie's Fledglings" or "The Young Guns"?

17 David left home in London for Manchester at the age of 16, 18 or 19?

18 David led six-year-old Kirsty Howard out on to the pitch for an England match against which country?

19 David scored two goals in Manchester United's January 1998 5-3 FA Cup win against which London team?

20 Aged 11, David was booed at Old Trafford by Tottenham fans, because he supported Manchester United: true or false?

21 Did David or Victoria once play the lead in a school production of *The Pied Piper*?

22 Which Manchester United midfield hero was Middlesbrough manager in the late 1990s?

23 Malcolm Fidgeon was David's PE teacher, the Manchester United scout who signed David or Sir Alex Ferguson's first assistant manager?

24 At Le Tournoi, David got a yellow card for not getting on a stretcher: true or false?

25 Whose name is stitched into David's boots above the name of his first son?

MATCH FIT 2

Match the nicknames to the teams that David has played against. **(See answers on p146.)**

The Gunners	West Bromwich Albion
The Owls	Arsenal
The Canaries	Leicester City
The Toffees	Derby County
The Saints	Sheffield Wednesday
The Black Cats	Norwich
The Hammers	Southampton
The Baggies	West Ham United
The Foxes	Sunderland
The Rams	Everton

Move these letters around to discover
some of David's England team-mates.
(See answers on p149.)

```
D P I E N E D E W S T S
U O D T J O C I X E M O
U L W X R P E N J G I H
Y A N I T N E G R A O O
A N D P I F D Y Y L P L
H D G A O Y N W L O U I
Q F R J G A L A X U P Z
M K F R M R N A I O I A
U V B R V D E L T Y P R
J J E B A V S E J I Y B
B G A I N O D E C A M X
A L B A N I A I B E T R
L C X X C O L O M B I A
L X A V O D L O M V C S
```

Albania	Greece	Moldova
Argentina	Holland	Poland
Brazil	Italy	Sweden
Colombia	Macedonia	Ukraine
Germany	Mexico	

(See answers on p151.)

1   Which family member of David's accidentally hit a fan in the head when celebrating David's first goal in European competition?

2   How many decades (tens of years) had Manchester United been unbeaten at home in European competitions?

3   In the 1996-1997 season, David scored when Manchester United beat which Turkish team in Turkey: Galatasaray, Fenerbahce or Besiktas?

4   Was Manchester United's first Premiership game of the 2002-2003 season against West Bromwich Albion, West Ham or Wimbledon?

5   David was playing for Ridgeway Rovers, Chingford United or Waltham Forest when he was spotted by a Manchester United scout before he was a teenager?

6   Which ground that David has frequently played at is on the road called Sir Matt Busby Way?

7 Sandra Georgina West is the name of David's mother, David's sister or David's aunt?

8 How many games did David play in the 1997 Le Tournoi tournament?

9 David tends to hit his free kicks with a ten pace run-up, a seven pace run-up or a two or three step run-up?

10 What item of her clothing did Victoria say David wore but was actually, only joking?

11 Which country played England in England for the first time in 2002?

12 In what year was he first picked to play a full international for England?

13 David fell for Victoria whilst watching a Spice Girls video on TV but in which country: France, Spain, Georgia or the United States?

14 Which team-mate of David's made his England debut in Le Tournoi against Italy?

15 David provided the pass to which English player who put England ahead 2-1 in the 1998 World Cup game against Argentina?

16 Louis Malloy is: David's publicity agent, a referee that once sent him off or the creator of David's first tattoo?

17 Which Manchester United team-mate decided against having a tattoo after David had one?

18 What was the score in the 1998 England v Argentina game after extra time?

19 David became the PFA Young Player of the Year but in which year?

20 David's first car was a bright yellow Ford Anglia: true or false?

21 Against which country did he first captain England?

22 'Out of Your Mind' was Victoria's first, second or third solo single?

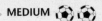

23 Beckham scored the winner in his first ever game for Manchester United: true or false?

24 David contributed to a charity book of poems called *Hug 'O War*. Did the proceeds from the book go to help orphans in Romania, Kosovo or Ethiopia?

25 What two English competitions when won together are known as "doing the double"?

MATCH FIT 3

Match the Premiership managers with clubs they managed during the 2002-2003 season. **(See answers on p147.)**

Peter Reid	West Bromwich Albion
Arsene Wenger	Aston Villa
Sam Allardyce	Everton
Gordon Strachan	Liverpool
Sir Bobby Robson	Bolton Wanderers
David Moyes	West Ham
Gary Megson	Sunderland
Graham Taylor	Newcastle United
Gerard Houllier	Southampton
Glen Roeder	Arsenal

1   Beckham's first game of the 1998-1999 season was against LKS Lodz, Leicester City or West Ham?

2   David's ex-team-mate, Dwight Yorke, joined Manchester United from which football club?

3   Which ex-manager of Manchester United was nicknamed "The Doc"?

4   The ten male workers of the Bengal Dynasty restaurant in Clywd all shaved their heads in tribute to David Beckham: true or false?

5   David and Victoria's mansion in Hertfordshire was built in the 1800s, the 1930s or the 1990s?

6   David's first goal of the 1998-1999 season came from a free kick, penalty, header or long shot?

7   After playing in the 2-2 draw against Greece, David's next match was against a Greek club side: true or false?

8 Was Robbie Savage a member of the Manchester United youth team at the same time as David?

9 In the summer of 1997, David was part of an England team that played in what competition?

10 The former assistant to Sir Alex Ferguson, Bryan Kidd, left to become manager of which football club?

11 Which World Cup-winning defender is a team-mate of David's?

12 Victoria met which other Spice Girl whilst auditioning for a film in 1994?

13 David was one of 3, 43 or 103 boys who turned up for trials to Ridgeway Rovers Under-8s team?

14 Which rival of Manchester United plays its home games at Stamford Bridge?

15 Gary and Phil Neville were selected for England squads long before David got a call-up: true or false?

16   David's first son, Brooklyn, was named after a part of which American city?

17   How many times had an England team beaten Germany in Germany before 2001?

18   In the 2000-2001 Champions League did Manchester United reach the quarter-finals, semi-finals or final?

19   David Beckham has a deal with Rage to make computer games, clothing, jewellery or sarongs?

20   Former Arsenal winger Graham Rix was in charge of which team David was made captain of?

21   Which one of the following did David not date: Lisa Rhys-Halska, Sophie Ellis-Bextor, Leoni Marzell or Belinda Gibson?

22   David scored once, twice or three times in Manchester United's 5-1 thrashing of Wimbledon in 1998?

23 In which country was the 1999 Champions League final?

24 David's eldest sister used to play football for England Schoolgirls: true or false?

25 Both of Manchester United's 1999 Champions League final goals were scored after 89 minutes: true or false?

CROSSING PUZZLE 1

Solve the clues to spell out the surname of a former manager of David's, by using the first letter of each answer. (See answers on p148.)

- The name given to three goals scored by the same player.

- The surname of England's top striker who plays for Liverpool.

- A way of restarting play which begins with the referee letting go of the ball.

- Moving the football under close control with a series of small touches.

- The full first name of the footballing cousin of David's team-mate Rio Ferdinand.

- The number of players in a football team.

Play against a friend, taking turns to read out and answer the questions. If the scores are level after five questions each, whoever gets closest to the sudden death question is the winner.

(See answers on p145.)

Penalty Shootout 2

A1 When David battled against Luis Figo in midfield, which country was he playing against?

B1 Which international team was he playing against when facing Rivaldo and Roberto Carlos?

A2 How often are the World Cup finals held?

B2 How often are the European Championships held?

A3 From what competition did Manchester United withdraw and receive much criticism?

B3 Can you name the former Aston Villa goalkeeper signed after Peter Schmeichel left Manchester United?

A4 Against which team was the first game David and England played in the 2000 European Championships?

B4 Against which team with City in their name did David score an 80th minute penalty in the 2002-2003 Worthington Cup competition?

A5 Which African team did England play in a friendly in Japan shortly before the 2002 World Cup?

B5 David played in an England friendly against which island nation found in the Mediterranean Sea?

Sudden Death Question

What is the most number of goals Manchester United have scored in a league season?

1. Which team did Manchester United face in the 1999 Champions League final?

2. Which two clubs that both have "Valley" in their ground name has David played at?

3. David's ex-team-mate, Andy Cole, joined Manchester United from which football club?

4. What was the Spice Girls' first hit single?

5. Beckham was substituted in Manchester United's 5-1 win over Wimbledon. Which son of a famous Dutch footballer replaced him?

6. In September 1998, David scored a great free kick against which Spanish football club?

7. In what month did he get married: March, July, September or October?

8. Which spoof chat show host interviewed David and his wife?

9   The Japan Travel Bureau is organising Beckham tours of England: true or false?

10 Are David, Nicky Butt and Paul Scholes all the same age?

11 Against which team did David miss his first game of the 1998-1999 season: Brondby, Spurs, Chelsea or Leeds United?

12 At what stadium was the 1999 FA Cup final held?

13 What was the score at the end of the first half of the England v Argentina game in 1998?

14 One of David's midfield heroes, Bryan Robson, was signed to Manchester United from which club?

15 Did David join Ridgeway Rovers through a newspaper advert, television advert or a personal invitation?

16 David's father-in-law has the same name as a former England team captain. What is it?

17 After signing his first boot contract, did David buy a red leather coat, a blue Porsche or a gold necklace?

18 In the treble-winning season of 1999, what was the last trophy Manchester United won: Champions League, FA Cup or the Premiership?

19 Le Tournoi saw England and David play Brazil, France and which other European nation?

20 In a Manchester United training match, in August 1997, between the older and younger players, who was in goal for the young players?

21 In October 1997, Manchester United thrashed Barnsley. Was the score: 5-0, 6-0, 7-0 or 8-0?

22 Manchester United were placed in Group A, B, C, D or E in the 1998-1999 Champions League?

23   How old was David when he signed
      as a schoolboy to Manchester United?

24   What is the name of Victoria's
      company: Moon Productions, Moody
      Productions or Move Productions?

25   Which team did Manchester United
      face in the semi-final of the
      Worthington Cup in 2003?

FIRST HALF 8

1   Did Dwight Yorke join David and the
     other members of the Manchester
     United team for six million, nine
     million or over twelve million pounds?

2   Which team did Manchester United
     play three times in the 1998-1999
     Champions League?

3   Which former defender team-mate
     used to blame David's crosses for not
     scoring goals: Jaap Stam, Ronny
     Johnsen or Steve Bruce?

4 Which youth team-mate of David's was an Irish winger who moved to Newcastle United?

5 Gary Neville's father and mother both worked for many years at which north-western football club?

6 In what place did David come in the nationwide Bobby Charlton Soccer Skills Tournament?

7 Is Victoria's brother, Christian, younger or older than her?

8 From which country were the teams Manchester United had to beat in the quarter-finals and semi-finals of the 1998-1999 Champions League?

9 At the end of the 1998-1999 Premiership season, which team came second behind Manchester United?

10 David and Victoria organised a giant pre-World Cup party in 2002. Was the theme and food: Japanese, Spanish, French or Italian?

11   David's first game in the Champions
     League was against a team from
     Turkey, Switzerland, France or
     Belgium?

12   Which now-famous midfielder for
     Manchester United could not make it
     into their 1992 FA Youth Cup side?

13   Which team did Manchester United
     defeat in David's first ever FA Cup
     final appearance?

14   David was part of the team
     responsible for winning which trophy
     in 1992?

15   Against which team did he score his
     first World Cup finals goal?

16   What did David and Victoria
     announce in January 1998?

17   What was the name of the movie that
     the Spice Girls made?

18   Is David's favourite music: jazz, rap,
     pop or rock?

19 How old was David when he saw news of a competition about the search for the best young footballer in the country on the TV show, *Blue Peter*?

20 What club other than Manchester United did he have a trial for as a schoolboy?

21 In 2002, David received a world record number of birthday emails, Christmas cards or anniversary presents?

22 In which two countries were the 2002 World Cup finals held?

23 Gary Peters managed David for a short period at which football club?

24 David was substituted in an England game against Saudi Arabia: true or false?

25 After England were knocked out, which team went on to win the 1998 World Cup?

1 David accidentally hit a young
   Leicester fan in the face with a shot
   during a 1997 game. Did he give his
   shirt, an autograph or his boots to
   the fan after the match?

2 Malcolm Fidgeon organised for David
   to have a trial with Manchester
   United or appear on TV as an eleven
   year old?

3 In what season did Manchester
   United face three teams in their
   Champions League group all
   beginning with the letter, B?

4 On what famous aircraft did David
   and the rest of the Manchester
   United squad fly to reach the 1999
   Champions League final?

5 Did Beckham play on the right of
   midfield, the centre of midfield or as
   a striker in the 1999 FA Cup final?

6 "The Guvnor" was the nickname of
   which former team-mate of David's:
   Steve Bruce, Mark Hughes or Paul
   Ince?

7 In a one week stay in Georgia for an England match, David ran up a phone bill of: £160, £400, £800 or £1,600?

8 Which England manager resigned after losing 1-0 to Germany in 2000?

9 Which member of the *Match of the Day* TV show called David's mohican haircut "absurd"?

10 David was booked in both of his 1997 Le Tournoi games: true or false?

11 David scored in a 2-2 draw against a European team in October 2002. Can you name them?

12 A giant plaster cast of David's injured foot was auctioned to help which of the following charities: NSPCC, Greenpeace or Oxfam?

13 In September 2001, Manchester United and Newcastle United scored a total of seven goals in a game. What was the score?

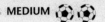

14 How many qualifying games for the 1998 World Cup did England play?

15 How many of those games did David play in?

16 In what year was David's first ever game for the full Manchester United team: 1990, 1992, 1994 or 1996?

17 Which Spanish club did David visit as an eleven year old?

18 Who bought David a Ferrari 550 as a birthday present?

19 Which member of the England 2002 World Cup plays his club football in Germany?

20 How many days after getting engaged did David ask a footballer to be his best man at his wedding?

21 In a 1998 international against Belgium, which famous Geordie midfield player did David replace when he came on as a substitute?

22 Which 2002 Manchester United team-mate scored for the opposition in the penalty shootout that knocked England out of the 1998 World Cup?

23 In which English county would you find 'Beckingham Palace'?

24 In which two countries was the 2000 European Championships held?

25 Is Michael Jordan, Michael Owen, Michael Jackson or Michael Parkinson, David's greatest hero?

MATCH FIT 4

Match the Champions League teams to their country. **(See answers on p147.)**

Barcelona	France
Bayern Munich	Italy
FC Basle	Spain
PSV Eindhoven	Croatia
Paris St. Germain	Norway
Rosenborg	Germany
Dinamo Zagreb	Switzerland
Deportivo La Coruna	Sweden
Parma	Holland
IFK Gothenburg	Spain

1   David's friends, Gary and Phil Neville, have a sister who plays for England at what sport?

2   On 24 January 1998, David got married, won the FA Cup or got engaged?

3   What is Victoria's nickname for David, which she admitted on the *Parkinson* chat show?

4   Which one of the following stars did not attend David and Victoria's pre-World Cup party in 2002: Jamie Oliver, Mick Jagger or Gary Lineker?

5   In 2001, David came second, third or fourth in FIFA's World Footballer of the Year competition?

6   Which footballer with the first name, Luis, won the above competition?

7   What football club did David grow up just a short bus ride away from?

8   In which country were the 1998 World Cup finals held?

9   David had a car crash in 2002 whilst driving his car with his foot in plaster: true or false?

10   David's first game for a full Manchester United team ended in a 1-1 draw, a 2-1 win or a 3-2 defeat?

11   David's second goal for Preston was against Fulham, Rotherham, Crewe or Wolves?

12   An 85-year-old grandmother had a Beckham mohican haircut in 2001: true or false?

13   Which country would David be playing against if his shot was saved by his Manchester United team-mate Fabien Barthez?

14   Jesper Blomqvist came to Manchester United from Parma in Italy but what country is he originally from?

15   Which member of the Manchester United 2001-2002 team came from Argentina?

16 Who did the Manchester United youth team play in the final of the 1993 FA Youth Cup?

17 Which team topped the 1998 World Cup Group A ensuring that England had to face Argentina?

18 World Sight Day was a charity event supported by David, Gary Neville and which other Manchester United player?

19 The German scorer of the winning goal against England in 2000 plays for which rival of Manchester United?

20 In 1999, Sir Alex Ferguson fined David how much for being out late at night?

21 Which country does Luis Figo come from?

22 How many members were there of the original Spice Girls?

23 David went to see Oasis but which football team do Oasis support?

24 The 1995-96 season was David's first playing regularly for Manchester United. Did the season start with a win, draw or defeat?

25 Which former team-mate of David's was banned after kicking a spectator at a game against Crystal Palace?

FIRST HALF 11

1 David won BBC Sports Personality of the Year in 2001. Which Liverpool footballer came third?

2 David played for Manchester United in the Champions League before he had ever played in the Premiership: true or false?

3 On BBC Radio One, which ex-Manchester United footballer did Beckham list as one of his heroes?

4 Which current member of the Manchester United side has captained Ireland?

5   When he was two years old, Brooklyn Beckham was offered an official football contract: true or false?

6   Who was the second England manager David played under?

7   David captained England to a 3-0 win in 2001 against which European team?

8   Which famous football pundit said, "You don't win anything with kids", about the young Manchester United side featuring David?

9   Which ex-Manchester United team-mate of David's was in goal for Manchester City when City won 3-1 in 2002?

10 After what incident did David cry for ten minutes when with his parents?

11 David was the first man to appear on the front cover of *Company* magazine for 5, 10, 15 or 25 years?

12 In the games David played for Preston North End, how many times were they beaten?

13 Robert de Niro's character in the movie, *Taxi Driver*, was the inspiration for which of David's famous haircuts?

14 David scored one of England's goals in a 4-0 win in 2001 but against which team?

15 Which Manchester United player did the 11-year-old David get the autograph of at Barcelona?

16 David was asked to leave his second lodgings in Manchester after breaking the television: true or false?

17 David's dad's football nickname was "the offside king" for being offside more than other players: true or false?

18 Did David and Victoria celebrate their second wedding anniversary with a visit to the cinema, a Chinese restaurant or the opera?

19 England's professional footballers voted David the Young Player of the Year in 1994, 1997, 1999 or 2001?

20 What song featuring Frank Skinner and David Baddiel became the most popular England song for supporters from 1996 onwards?

21 Who was manager of the England team when David took part in the 2000 European Championships?

22 In the season before the 1998 World Cup, David made less than 10, less than 25, less than 40 or more than 50 appearances for Manchester United?

23 The player David was sent off for kicking in the 1998 World Cup, was unpunished, also sent off or given a yellow card?

24 David turned down acting as a hitman in the movie *Red Light Runners*: true or false?

25 David made a mistake which led to Kevin Nolan scoring the winner in a September 2002 match. What was the name of the winning team?

CROSSING PUZZLE 2

*Solve the clues to spell out the name of someone near and dear to David, by using the first letter of each answer. (**See answers on p148.**)*

- The surname of an Australian centre forward who played for Leeds and has the first name, Marc.

- The name of the East Anglian team who play at Portman Road.

- To kick a ball from the wing to midfield.

- The way the ball is brought back into play when it has crossed the sidelines.

- The name given to the sort of goal scored when you put the ball past your team's goalkeeper.

- The surname of the husband of pop star Louise and a former Liverpool midfielder.

- A type of free kick.

- The second name of the football club whose first is Charlton.

SECOND HALF

1. In which month in 2002 was his second son born?

2. In July 2002, David caused a stir by appearing in public with his fingernails painted what colour?

3. At which English league ground was the England v Mexico game of 2001 played?

4. David's grandfather, Joseph West, was a season ticket holder at which London football club?

5. Which Manchester United team-mate's house was David at when he received the phone call telling him he would captain for the first time?

6 Which member of David's family suggested that he swap shirts with Diego Simeone when they next played against each other?

7 In the 1998 World Cup game against Argentina, was David sent off in the first or second half?

8 David's dad was a gas engineer, a tailor or a professional footballer?

9 David played at Manchester United with the 2002-2003 manager of Wales. Who is he?

10 The Westin Awaji Island Resort is where David and the rest of the England team stayed during 1998 World Cup, 2002 World Cup or the 2000 European Championships?

11 David got booked, sent off or scored a hat-trick against Mexican champions, Nexaca in 2000?

12 Which team did England face in their very last match at the old Wembley Stadium?

13 Is the number tattooed on David found on his back, arm or leg?

14 How often does he like to change his football boots to a new pair: once a season, once a month or for every game?

15 In what division were the team David went on loan to in the 1994-1995 season?

16 Was David the smallest, tallest or fattest member of the Ridgeway Rovers junior team?

17 Manchester United won a FIFA World Club Championship game against a football club from Australia: true or false?

18 The newspaper headline: "3 Lions On My Skirt" referred to what item of clothing David was photographed wearing?

19 Was David's first goal as England captain against Finland, Ireland or Brazil?

20 Who managed England for the next game after Kevin Keegan resigned?

21 England beat Finland 2-1 in the 2002 World Cup qualifiers but at what English ground was the game held?

22 In which year was David runner-up in the BBC Sports Personality of the year?

23 In 1993, David and the Manchester United youth team won, came second or were knocked out in the quarter-finals of the FA Youth Cup?

24 In 1999, Manchester United won two, three or four competitions?

25 David Beckham is a quarter Hindi: true or false?

SECOND HALF 2

1 Ridgeway Rovers went unbeaten for one, two or three seasons?

2   Who won the 2001-2002 Premiership
    title: Arsenal, Manchester United or
    Leeds?

3   Diego Simeone and David Beckham
    met in what competition after the
    1998 World Cup?

4   Which team did David and the rest
    of the England team beat for the
    first time in 34 years in the 2000
    European Championships?

5   David faced France in a Le Tournoi
    game in 1997. Did England win, lose
    or draw?

6   England's friendly against Portugal
    in 2002 was held at: The Stadium
    of Light, Villa Park, St Mary's Stadium
    or Old Trafford?

7   On BBC Radio One, which famous
    American boxer did David state was
    one of his heroes?

8   David played three league cup games
    in 1994-1995. Two were against Port
    Vale. Who was the third against?

9   Against which Yorkshire team was David's last Premiership game of the 2001-2002 season?

10 David's mother's father is Jewish, a Hindu, a Muslim or a Catholic?

11 How many games did David play for Preston North End whilst on loan?

12 Manchester United won the first Manchester derby match of the 2000-2001 season. Was the second a defeat, win or draw for David's team?

13 Is David's favourite TV comedy: *Only Fools and Horses*, *Birds of a Feather*, *The Office* or *Blackadder*?

14 Who won the 2000-2001 Premiership title: Arsenal, Manchester United or Leeds?

15 Argentinean Pedro Duscher's tackle broke David's collar bone, toe or shin bone?

16 What competition did David and Manchester United win in 1992?

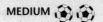

17 David and Victoria have two dogs, rabbits, cats or parrots as pets?

18 The England manager, Sven-Goran Eriksson, has previously managed: Liverpool, Lazio, Leeds United or Lincoln City?

19 Germany beat England in 2000 in Germany, at Wembley Stadium or the Millennium Stadium?

20 A foul on which England player gave the free kick from which David scored the equalising goal against Greece in 2001?

21 Which member of the Spice Girls left in 1998?

22 David scored one goal in Manchester United's February 2002 5-1 win over which French team?

23 What name can be found displayed on David's golf shoes?

24 David signed a deal with Sondico to endorse which item of football kit?

25 David's first car was a Ford Escort, a Vauxhall Cavalier, a Lotus Espirit or a VW Beetle?

SECOND HALF 3

1 Who first made Beckham captain of England?

2 He has played for one other English league team apart from Manchester United: which one was it?

3 Mark Niblett was David and Victoria's butler, business manager or cook?

4 At what ground was the England v Greece match held in the 2002 World Cup warm ups?

5 What royal nickname is given to David's mansion?

6 Victoria auditioned in 1994, but failed to get a part in which of the following movies: *Tank Girl, Tomb Raider, Spiderman* or *GI Jane*?

7 David's first games were for a Sunday League team that was organised by who?

8 Against which team was England's biggest win in the 2002 World Cup?

9 Was Beckham's goal against Greece in 2001 a free kick, penalty or header?

10 At a trial for which football club did David turn up wearing a Manchester United shirt?

11 DB07 is David's first venture into computer games, a clothing range or a new football boot?

12 Jackie and Tony are David or Victoria's parents' names?

13 Did David make his debut for England in 1995, 1996, 1997 or 1998?

14 In October 1999, Manchester United flew out to play Sturm Graz in the Champions League. In what country do Sturm Graz play?

15 What sort of breed are the Beckham's dogs, Puffy and Snoop?

16 As a teenager, David worked at Walthamstow Greyhound Track: true or false?

17 David was dropped for the top-of-the-table clash with which team in February 2000 after missing training?

18 Which of these cars does David not own: Aston Martin, BMW Series 5 or Lincoln Navigator?

19 Whose number seven shirt did Beckham take at Manchester United?

20 Which of the following were not members of David's wife's band: Geri Halliwell, Holly Valance, Emma Bunton or Nicole Appleton?

21 Which other player made his England debut in the same game as David Beckham: Andy Hinchcliffe, Sol Campbell or Alan Shearer?

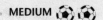

22 Against which team was England's first 2002 World Cup match?

23 David Beckham was born in Leytonstone, Salford or Edinburgh?

24 What number has David had tattooed on himself?

25 David Beckham is the name of a meatball dish served in Bangkok in Thailand: true or false?

MATCH FIT 5

Match the European teams David has faced to their grounds. **(See answers on p148.)**

Barcelona	Constant Vanden Stock
Internazionale	Velodrome Stadium
Bayer Leverkusen	Artemio Franchi
Olympiakos	San Siro
Galatasaray	Olympic Stadium
Fiorentina	Bernabeu
Real Madrid	BayArena
Dynamo Kiev	Nou Camp
Anderlecht	Ali Semi Yen
Marseilles	Lefkosia

Play against a friend, taking turns to read out and answer the questions. If the scores are level after five questions each, whoever gets closest to the sudden death question is the winner.

(See answers on p145.)

Penalty Shootout 3

A1 Which manager appointed David as vice-captain for the England team?

B1 Against which European team did England, featuring David, win 6-0 in 1999?

A2 In the 1999-2000 season, how many goals did he score in 31 league appearances?

B2 How many bookings did David obtain in total in the 2001-2002 season?

A3 David was made the PFA Young Player of the Year in 1994, 1997 or 1999?

B3 David made 33, 43 or 73 appearances in the 2001-2002 season?

A4 Which north-western team inflicted Manchester United's first defeat of the 2002-2003 season?

B4 England played two qualifying games for the Euro 2004 Championships in October 2002. Did David play in one, both or neither?

A5 How many goals did Manchester United score in their two games against Brondby in 1998?

B5 Who knocked Manchester United out of the 1998-1999 Worthington Cup?

Sudden Death Question

Before the Bayer Leverkusen game in November 2002, how many league games including substitutions had David played for Manchester United?

1 Which Italian club did Jaap Stam leave Manchester United to join?

2 David's son appeared as a cartoon in the 3000th issue of which comic: *The Beano, WWF Superstars, The Dandy* or *The X-Men*?

3 Against which team did Beckham score a penalty in the 2002 World Cup?

4 In what year did he get married?

5 The Old School House is the name of David's house, his parents' house or Victoria's parents' house?

6 Which acts has Victoria not sung in or with: Spice Girls, Ash, True Steppers or Atomic Kitten?

7 Against which team did England play their last 2002 World Cup qualifying match?

8 Can you name one of Beckham's team-mates who scored more goals than him in the 2001-2002 season?

9 Which team-mate's own goal did David equalise when playing Sunderland on New Year's Day 2003?

10 Caroline McAteer was Victoria's publicity agent, David's personal trainer, a member of the Spice Girls or David's ex-girlfriend?

11 David's father-in-law used to be in a sixties band called The Sonics: true or false?

12 How many yellow cards did David receive in the 2002 World Cup?

13 David's father-in-law asked for a song to be played as Victoria and David drove to their wedding. Was it by Stevie Wonder, the Beatles, the Spice Girls or Robbie Williams?

14 Was David playing a Spanish, Italian or German team when he broke his toe before the 2002 World Cup?

15 Did he collect his 50th England cap before, during or after the 2002 World Cup?

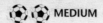

16   How many games did David play in
      the 2002 World Cup?

17   What sport (not football) has David
      said he would like Brooklyn to
      become a star at?

18   Manchester United's new training
      ground is at Carrington, Davyhulme,
      Stretford or Chester?

19   In what year did Manchester United
      first win the Champions League?

20   Which one of the following has not
      managed David in the England team:
      Glenn Hoddle, Graham Taylor,
      Howard Wilkinson or Kevin Keegan?

21   Micah Hyde beat David to the
      Ridgeway Rovers player of the year
      trophy two years in a row: true or
      false?

22   Goff's Oak is the childhood home of
      David, Victoria or Sir Alex Ferguson?

23   In what year did David first captain
      England in a full international match?

24 What is the four letter name of the TV channel dedicated to Manchester United on which David appears in interviews?

25 David's mother-in-law used to work as a jazz singer, a hairdresser, a photographer or a teacher?

SECOND HALF 5

1 Which Manchester United legend was the first to spot David's talent: George Best, Sir Bobby Charlton or Lou Macari?

2 Beckham became UEFA's Player of the Year in 1997, 1999 or 2000?

3 Who was the player that David Beckham kicked when he was sent off in the 1998 World Cup: Diego Simeone, Gabriel Batistuta or Claudio Lopez?

4 David has two brothers, two sisters or is an only child?

5 Between 1996 and 2001, there was only one year in which Manchester United did not win a trophy – which year was it?

6 What competition did David and Manchester United win in 2000?

7 In 1986, David met the Barcelona team, which included which English striker and crisp thief?

8 As a trainee in Manchester, David was asked to leave his first lodgings because: he stayed out late, he stole money or another boy took food from the kitchen?

9 David appeared in *The Face* magazine with a mohican haircut but in which year?

10 What was the nationality of the player whose tackle broke David's toe in 2002?

11 Victoria's first band was called Persuasion, The Delighted, The Pretty Things or As If By Magic?

12 The first England manager David worked under now manages which Premiership club?

13 Who did David and Kirsty Howard hand the torch to at the opening ceremony of the Commonwealth Games in 2002?

14 Which previous England captain also wore the Manchester United number seven shirt in the 1980s?

15 "WANTED – Football Stars of the Future" was the start of an advert for players to join Manchester United, Ridgeway Rovers, Preston or Waltham Forest?

16 David's family received abusive telephone calls after he was sent off in the 1998 World Cup: true or false?

17 David signed as a youth trainee with Manchester United in 1990, 1991, 1992 or 1993?

18 What team did David support as a youngster?

19 Old Trafford football ground has a nickname including the word, "theatre". Can you name it?

20 In which country is a statue of David part of a Buddhist temple: England, Thailand, China or Korea?

21 How many games was David Beckham substituted in the 2002 World Cup?

22 David's first goal for Preston was from a corner which went straight in: true or false?

23 Victoria went to the Laine Arts Theatre School, Essex University or Birmingham Drama College after leaving school?

24 How old was David when he captained England for the first time?

25 How many people turned up when David accompanied his wife on a promotional stop at a Woolworths store in Oldham: 60, 600 or 6,000?

1   David has an apartment near Manchester. Is it situated in Urmston, Cheadle, Alderley Edge or Worsley?

2   A twelve-inch high statue of David is part of Bangkok's Pariwas Temple: true or false?

3   Luttrellstown Castle was the scene of David and Victoria's wedding, where he received the Footballer of the Year award or where he first met Sir Alex Ferguson?

4   David's father-in-law is called Tony Adams: true or false?

5   Which former team-mate at Manchester United was a striker who played for Trinidad and Tobago?

6   David's hair changed dramatically in March 2000 to a mohican, a number two shaved cut or a perm?

7   A pair of his football boots were auctioned and fetched over £13,000: true or false?

8 David used to play cricket for Essex juniors: true or false?

9 Who called David back early from his honeymoon for football training?

10 Against which team did David make his first appearance for Manchester United?

11 What is the title of the book about David featuring photographs from Dean Freeman?

12 Stuart Underwood managed David whilst he played at Ridgeway Rovers, Preston North End or the Manchester United youth team?

13 Did David score 41, 61, 71 or 101 goals in three seasons as a youngster?

14 Whose illness prompted David to miss morning training before the Leeds United game in February 2000?

15 What is David's favourite US basket-ball team: the Utah Jazz, the LA Lakers or the Chicago Bulls?

16   Against which team was Manchester United's last competitive match of the 1998-1999 season?

17   Which team-mate of David's dated supermodel, Linda Evangelista?

18   David Beckham's appearance against Bayer Leverkusen was his 68th European appearance, a record he tied with which friend?

19   In the 2000-2001 season, did David score a total of 9, 11, 16 or 23 goals for Manchester United?

20   The England manager in a 0-0 draw with Finland was appointed as Sunderland manager in 2002. What is his name?

21   The second car that David owned was a Volkswagen Golf, a Ford Capri or a Peugeot 206?

22   David's father had trials with which one of these professional football clubs: West Ham, Leyton Orient, Brighton and Hove Albion or Millwall?

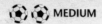

23 At which Scottish club had Sir Alex Ferguson had European success before managing Manchester United?

24 Tyler is the name of David's favourite hair stylist, rap artist or tattooist?

25 Victoria grew up in Goff's Oak and her family were the only house with: a garden, a swimming pool, security guards or a helicopter landing pad?

 SECOND HALF 7

1 Against which team was David playing in 1996 when he scored a stunning 57 yard goal?

2 Beckham played alongside which gifted French player in the 1996 season?

3 In 1996, David captained the England Under 17, England Under 21 or the full England team?

4   Which of these two FA Youth Cup finals did Manchester United win: the 1992 or 1993?

5   Arsene Wenger has managed Arsenal longer than Sir Alex Ferguson has managed Manchester United: true or false?

6   Which film with David's surname in the title features a female Indian footballer called Jess?

7   Which Manchester United team-mate became manager of Birmingham City and led them back into the Premiership?

8   The goalkeeper, Peter Schmeichel, comes from Holland, France, Denmark or Sweden?

9   In a 1999 questionnaire, what sort of takeaway food did David say is his favourite?

10 David and Victoria watched the Kirov Ballet at the Royal Opera House in 2001: true or false?

11 David has his left ear, right ear or both ears pierced?

12 Was Mark Wood, David's first football manager, Victoria's ex-boyfriend or David's team-mate in the Manchester United youth team?

13 At what sort of sports event in America did David meet movie stars, Dustin Hoffman and Jack Nicholson?

14 In what year was he voted BBC Sports Personality of the year?

15 David's debut for Manchester United was in the league, FA Cup or Rumbelows Cup?

16 Kim Neilsen was a former school-teacher, a referee who sent David off or a team-mate in the Manchester United youth team?

17 What hair cream company did David do advertising work for?

18 England won how many matches during the 1998 World Cup finals?

19   Victoria had worn a Manchester United kit for a photo shoot before meeting David: true or false?

20   Which England manager was the first to pick him for England?

21   Martin Edwards was the chairman, manager or youth team coach of Manchester United when David joined?

22   In what season was David part of the Manchester United team that won the FA Cup, the Champions League and the Premiership?

23   Which other United did Manchester United beat in the 1999 FA Cup final?

24   Beckham scored the winning goal after only two minutes in a 2000-2001 Premiership game against which team?

25   What part of his body did David injure in November 2002 thus missing games including against West Ham?

Sort out the letters to find some of David's former team-mates at Manchester United.

(See answers on p149.)

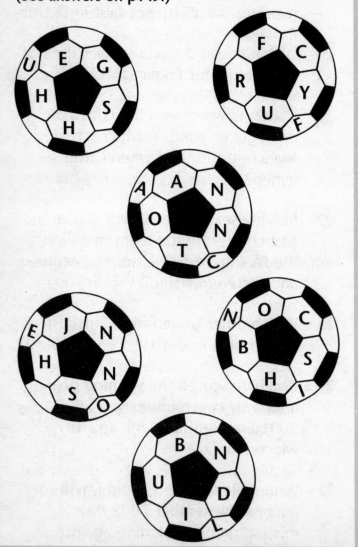

1   The Story of Beckham's Foot is now
    a course run by Queen Margaret
    University College in Edinburgh: true
    or false?

2   What was the amazing scoreline of
    England's 2001 game against
    Germany?

3   Which former Manchester United
    legend declared 11-year-old David as
    the best player of his age he'd seen
    in years?

4   Whilst playing for Essex, David's team
    lost 3-2 to Liverpool. Which young
    striker scored two of Liverpool's
    goals?

5   An ITV documentary about David
    showed him to be very neat and tidy,
    extremely untidy or reliant on a maid
    to tidy up after him?

6   David once left his wallet at a service
    station in Nottingham, Southampton
    or Manchester?

7   Against which team was his last
     Premiership match before suspension
     and injury in November 2002?

8   How many times has England won
     the World Cup?

9   For what soft drink did David and
     other international footballers play a
     game against sumo wrestlers in a TV
     advert?

10   Which football club did Victoria fight
     in 2002 for the right to the nickname
     "Posh"?

11   Against which team did David
     score his first goal in the qualifying
     campaign for the Euro 2004
     championships?

12   Who scored England's other goal in
     the 2-2 World Cup qualifying draw
     with Greece in 2002?

13   In what year was the kidnap plan on
     Victoria foiled: 1999, 2000, 2001 or
     2002?

14 Against which team did David score goals from free kicks in both the home and away games in the 2002 World Cup qualifiers?

15 What colour are David's eyes?

16 Which former England manager now manages David's local rival club, Manchester City?

17 In the 2000-2001 season which one of the following teams did David not score against: Bradford, QPR, Ipswich, West Ham or Coventry?

18 David's and Victoria's two dogs are named after football players, rap artists or classical musicians?

19 Which Manchester United player scored the winner in the first Manchester derby match of the 2000-2001 season?

20 Which Spanish side did Manchester United face in the second group stage of the 2002-2003 Champions League?

21   David's matches for Ridgeway Rovers were usually played on Saturday afternoons, Sunday mornings or Friday nights?

22   Which other team, beginning with the letter, A, completed England's 2002 World Cup qualifying group containing Germany, Greece and Finland?

23   David's entry in the charity book, *Hug O' War*, was 'Hey Diddle Diddle', 'Little Miss Muffet' or 'Humpty Dumpty'?

24   From which country does Manchester United striker, Diego Forlan come from?

25   Which coach, who has worked with David for many seasons, left to become the manager of Middlesbrough?

1   During the 2002 World Cup, which Japanese dish did the England team's hotel state as David's favourite: cucumber sushi, noodles or rice crackers?

2   When David first joined Manchester United, was he using Adidas, Reebok or Umbro football boots?

3   David found himself on the Old Trafford pitch in 1986 in a skills competition. Who did Manchester United draw 3-3 with in the game afterwards?

4   David is the eldest, middle or youngest child in his family?

5   Was a song called, "She Only Fancies Him Cos He Looks Like David Beckham": released as a single in 2000, sung as a joke on a comedy show or a track from Victoria's first album?

6   Is David 165cm, 175cm, 180cm, 185cm or 190cm tall?

7   At the opening ceremony of which athletics event in July 2002 did David make a surprise appearance?

8   Which Barcelona and England manager gave David the advice to practise all the time before he had become a teenager?

9   David's midfield team-mate, Roy Keane, joined Manchester United from which club?

10   In September 2002, Christopher Hawkins auctioned a pair of David's football boots he won in a competition. Did the boots sell for under a thousand, between one and two thousand or over two thousand pounds?

11   In what country was the Westin Awaji Island Resort in which David and the rest of the England squad stayed?

12   David broke his toe in 2002 against which team: Deportivo La Coruna, Real Madrid or Bayern Munich?

13 Victoria's father drove what sort of luxury car: a Ferrari, a Rolls Royce, a Mercedes or an Alfa Romeo?

14 How many times have Manchester United won the European Cup Winners Cup?

15 After his World Cup sending-off, a model of David was burned outside a pub in South London: true or false?

16 Which idol of David's was the first England manager to call him into the squad?

17 Which member of David's family donated the fee for David to attend the Bobby Charlton Soccer Skills Tournament?

18 Photos of his wedding first appeared in which of the following magazines: *Shoot, OK, Bella, Hello!* or *90 Minutes*?

19 David's prize for winning a skills contest was two weeks training with Barcelona's youth team: true or false?

20 Which Manchester United team-mate did David first tell that he wanted Victoria to be his girlfriend?

21 The Spice Girls' manager, Simon Fuller, supported Arsenal, Manchester United or Liverpool?

22 David bought a Mercedes and tied it with a red bow as a Christmas present for whom?

23 For how long was David on loan at Preston North End: a week, a month, three months or a season?

24 Against which team did David make his first World Cup finals appearance in 1998?

25 In March 2000, a hair stylist travelled to Goff's Oak to give David a haircut but from where did he come?

1   David's first game back after his
    honeymoon was for England, for
    Manchester United in the FA Cup or
    in Manchester United's reserves?

2   David went on loan to Derby County
    for six weeks in the mid-1990s: true
    or false?

3   What sort of present did Victoria buy
    him for his 24th birthday: a ring, a
    sound system, a car or a new suit?

4   Which Italian club owed Manchester
    United £12 million for a transfer in
    2002?

5   David took Brooklyn to visit
    Disneyland but what US city is
    Disneyland in?

6   In what year did Sir Alex Ferguson
    become manager of Manchester
    United?

7   Which Englishman was manager of
    Barcelona when David visited the
    club as an eleven year old?

8 Shortly after beating Germany, David and Victoria appeared on a top TV chat show there. Did the audience boo, applaud or stay silent when they were on?

9 Victoria stayed in Ireland for a year as a tax exile: true or false?

10 David's family moved to Chingford where he attended the Chase Lane Junior School. In which English county is the school?

11 Which one of the following was not in the 1992 Manchester United youth team along with David: Nicky Butt, Gary Neville or Roy Keane?

12 Ali G's interview with David and Victoria was for which charity?

13 What country does David's club manager come from?

14 Which former team-mate of David's now plays in goal for local rivals, Manchester City?

15 In what competition in 2002 did David suffer a broken toe which nearly kept him out of the World Cup?

16 Who in a match against Belgium became England's youngest captain since 1963?

17 David's fifth yellow card in the 2002-2003 season meant that he missed a game against which local rivals in November 2002?

18 Winning the Fyfield five-a-side tournament was the occasion of what first for David: the first newspaper photo of him, his first medal or his first football contract?

19 Against Bayer Leverkusen in November 2002, Manchester United were down to ten men, because Beckham got sent off, another player got sent off or they got an injury after using all their substitutes?

20 Which Premiership team play their home games at St Mary's Stadium?

21 Who at Manchester United is the owner of the famous racehorse, Rock of Gibraltar?

22 Which Swiss side did Manchester United face in the second group stage of the 2002-2003 Champions League?

23 How many Manchester United players were in the England 2002 World Cup squad?

24 Against which European team did a Wales team featuring Ryan Giggs score a memorable win in October 2002?

25 According to FIFA statistics, how many shots on goal did David make in the 2002 World Cup?

Unscramble the letters to spell out the
name of a country that David has played
against. (See answers on p149.)

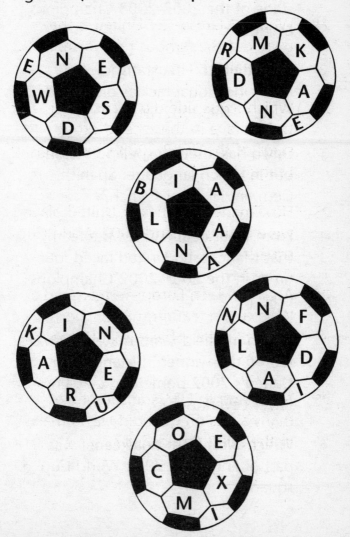

1   Which Italian side did Manchester United face in the second group stage of the 2002-2003 Champions League?

2   According to FIFA statistics, how many individual tackles did David make in the 2002 World Cup?

3   David has a tattoo spelling Victoria but in which language: Spanish, German, Hindi or French?

4   From what country was the team that Manchester United faced four times in the 2001-2002 Champions League?

5   Which midfield team-mate of David's scored the winner in Manchester United's 2002 home game against Bayer Leverkusen?

6   Which West Ham goalkeeper was part of England's 2002 World Cup squad?

7   *A Mind Of Its Own* is a book about Manchester United, a record of Victoria's or a documentary about David?

8   Which opposition team did David see play in the first Manchester United game he saw live?

9   Which Manchester United team-mate of David's played in central defence for England in the 2002 World Cup?

10   In what year did Manchester United win the UEFA Super Cup: 1978, 1991 or 1999?

11   In the 2002-2003 season, how many other Manchester United team-mates have a surname which starts with B?

12   Which Manchester United striker was signed from PSV Eindhoven in 2001?

13   Which close friend of David's did not recover from injury to join the 2002 World Cup squad?

14 David left his second lodgings in Manchester after complaining about the food, having a pillow fight or breaking a vase?

15 What is the middle name of David and Victoria's son, Romeo?

16 Which East European team beat England 2-0 in a friendly in November 1998?

17 Which TV celebrity asked the public to channel their energy to help David's broken toe to heal in time for the 2002 World Cup?

18 Which Manchester United player made 20 individual tackles for England in the 2002 World Cup?

19 In a Comfort survey, were David and Victoria voted most, second-most or least caring celebrity parents?

20 Which team did England play in their first game of the King Hassan II tournament?

21 In what year did Manchester United first win the FA Cup: 1909, 1939, 1969 or 1999?

22 What football team were first known as Newton Heath LYR?

23 David scored in his last match of 2002. Was it against Birmingham, Chelsea or West Ham?

24 Who did Manchester United beat in the 1994 Charity Shield competition?

25 David took over the right midfield position at Manchester United from: George Best, Andrei Kanchelskis or Ryan Giggs?

Play against a friend, taking turns to read out and answer the questions. If the scores are level after five questions each, whoever gets closest to the sudden death question is the winner.

(See answers on p145.)

Penalty Shootout 4

A1 In the year in which The Sun newspaper voted Ryan Giggs 34th best-looking man, what position was David?

B1 David Beckham used to frequently share hotel rooms for away games with which England player?

A2 Which former striker team-mate of David's moved to Aston Villa?

B2 Which ex-midfield team-mate of David's first moved to Liverpool and then Middlesbrough?

A3 Which is the only English football team Manchester United have played against in the UEFA Cup?

B3 Two baby birds at London Zoo were named after David and Victoria. What sort of bird were they?

A4 After being sent off in the England game, who did David phone for consolation?

B4 Which England defender had a goal disallowed in the 1998 World Cup game against Argentina?

A5 What is Victoria Beckham's star sign: Pisces, Aries, Scorpio or Taurus?

B5 What is David's star sign: Pisces, Aries, Scorpio or Taurus?

Sudden Death Question

How many times has Manchester United won the Division One and Premiership league titles?

TOUGH TO TACKLE

1. Name the part-time team David played against when he was demoted to the reserves in 1999?

2. How many England players were selected in all eight qualifying matches for the 1998 World Cup?

3. At which London football ground was David the Manchester United mascot in 1987?

4. As a youth trainee how much was he paid in expenses every week?

5. Matthew Barham, Ritchie Sutton and Danny Fielder are friends of David's from his time playing for Ridgeway Rovers, Preston North End or Chingford School?

6   Which team-mate of David's was nicknamed Kenny Dalglish as a youngster?

7   Which other Manchester United player had tried a shot from inside his own half the day David scored his 57 yard goal?

8   What was the name of the team that David first played for as an eight year old?

9   At Chingford High what nickname did his classmates give him?

10   In three seasons in the Enfield District team, how many goals did he score?

11   In 1986, David played a football competition in which European country?

12   What is the least number of games Manchester United have lost in a league season?

13   On which song of Victoria's did David sing some backing vocals?

14 David's 93rd minute swerved free kick gave Manchester United a draw on the 15 August 1998. Against which team was it scored?

15 In which month of 1998 did Manchester United score five goals in one game followed by six in the next?

16 Julie Killelea, an ex-girlfriend of David's, married which Manchester United team-mate?

17 Which player was picked to start the first game of the 1998 World Cup ahead of David?

18 Which team did David face when playing in the Arnold Schwarzenegger stadium?

19 David was booed heavily at which London club for his sending off in the 1998 World Cup?

20 How many months did Ian Denyer spend following David to make an ITV documentary about him?

21 Ellis Cashmore, the Professor of a course on David Beckham supports Aston Villa, Chelsea or Manchester United?

22 A number of David's team-mates all played for Boundary Park Juniors as children. Can you name one of the players?

23 In what year were Manchester United last relegated?

24 Manchester United beat a team from which country to qualify for the 1998-1999 Champions League?

25 In which season did David get his highest number of bookings?

⚽⚽⚽ TOUGH TO TACKLE 2 ⚽⚽⚽

1 How old was David when he first met Gary Neville?

2 Against whom did Manchester United record their highest ever victory?

3   Jim Peacock from Surrey claimed that David's face had appeared on what sort of chocolate biscuit?

4   In the early 1990s, Manchester United won the FA Youth Cup for the first time since 1964. Which team did they beat in the final?

5   David's last game for Preston and his first game for Manchester United in the league were both against teams beginning with the letter L. Can you name either of them?

6   Which David missed the final penalty shootout kick in the 1998 World Cup for England?

7   In what country was the FIFA World Club Championship 2000 held?

8   How many World Cup qualifying games had Germany lost in 61 matches before England beat them in 2001?

9   At what age did Victoria get engaged for the first time?

10   Which member of the England World
      Cup-winning team was in charge of
      the reserve players at Manchester
      United including David?

11   What event was voted the Golden TV
      Moment of 2001 by BBC viewers?

12   The referee for England's 2002 World
      Cup game with Nigeria was from the
      United States, Scotland or Australia?

13   Which Champions League opponents
      of Manchester United in 2002-2003,
      have a goalkeeper with the same
      surname as David's longtime
      team-mate, Nicky?

14   Who was David's partner in central
      midfield when Manchester United
      won the FA Youth Cup in 1992?

15   What was David's first squad number
      at Manchester United?

16   How many Premiership games did
      each team play in the 1993-1994
      season?

17 Which team-mate of David's scored the winner in the first Premiership game of the 2002-2003 season?

18 How many UK number one singles did the Spice Girls have?

19 Which Spanish team did David say that he'd most like to face in a European Cup final?

20 Lisa Rhys-Halska dated one other Manchester United player after David. Can you name him?

21 At what football ground beginning with the letter, S, did David score his 57 yard goal in 1996?

22 Which team beat Manchester United to the Premiership in the season that David played his first Premiership games?

23 What happened to David on 1 September 1996?

24 What threatening item was once sent to David with his name marked on it?

25 In David's England debut, which ex-Manchester United midfielder played alongside him?

CROSSING PUZZLE 3

*Solve the clues to find the surname of a footballing hero of David's, by using the first letter of each answer. (**See answers on p148.**)*

- The Brazilian who won FIFA World Player of the Year in 1997 and 1998.

- The name of the football team who play at Boundary Park.

- The surname of a former legendary manager of Manchester United who retired in 1969.

- The surname of a team-mate of David's ever since he joined Manchester United in 1991.

- To get unfairly in the way of an opposition player.

- The team that plays in North East England with the nickname, "The Magpies".

1. In the 2001-2002 season how many goals did David score in the Champions League?

2. What happened to David for the first time on 4 March 1999?

3. What is the lowest division Manchester United have played in?

4. David bought his sister what sort of car as a present?

5. In the 1999 Champions League final, David played in a team without Roy Keane and which other midfielder?

6. Before the 1990s, when was the last time Manchester United won the English league championship?

7. Tom Wood, Chingford High or Essex Academy was the name of the rival school to David's?

8. Which footballer passed the ball to David from which he scored his 1996 57 yard wonder goal?

9   According to footballer Brian McClair, David's mobile phone went off as who was giving a pre-match talk?

10   In which year did David start going out with Victoria?

11   David won a local athletics race four years in a row. What distance was the race in metres?

12   In what season did David make a staggering 62 appearances for club and country?

13   How many bookings did he receive in the 1995-1996 season?

14   David Edward Alan are the first and middle names of David, his brother or his father?

15   How old was David when he played his first football competition abroad?

16   The Spice Girls' second number one hit was 'Say You'll Be There', 'Wannabe' or 'Papa Don't Preach'?

17 Against which team did David make his full first team debut in the Premier League?

18 In May 2000, David and Victoria headed to which country for a holiday?

19 David was shown the red card in January 2000 but in which country were Manchester United playing at the time?

20 At which veteran pop star's south of France villa did he and Victoria spend some time before they were married?

21 When did the English Premiership start: 1988-1989, 1992-1993, 1994-1995 or 1997-1998?

22 In what Premiership season did Manchester United score their record 97 goals?

23 David and Victoria bought a mansion in Sawbridgeworth – how many bedrooms does it have?

24 In what year was Victoria born?

25 David was interviewed by Rage and said which team would he most like to face in an FA Cup final?

⚽⚽⚽ TOUGH TO TACKLE 4 ⚽⚽⚽

1 Music from which Disney film did David and Victoria choose as their entrance music to their wedding?

2 Against which team in 1999 did David and the rest of the Manchester United team suffer their worst defeat since 1996?

3 What was the score in the game above?

4 At what type of sports venue did David work as a 16 year old collecting glasses?

5 In the 2001-2002 season, how many goals did David score in the Premiership?

6 Manchester United drew against which Welsh team in a 2001 pre-season friendly?

7 Name the team-mate of David's who asked all female guests at his wedding to dress in Manchester United colours?

8 Which Manchester United youngster often replaces David on the right side of midfield?

9 As a youngster at Manchester United, what club car were he and others like Nicky Butt, given?

10 In one TV advert, he plays a game of table football against which Dutch footballer?

11 Which team did Manchester United score 8 goals against in 1999?

12 What was the name of the old Manchester United training ground that was formerly a racecourse?

13 What was David fined £800 for at a court in Stockport in 1999?

14 Which football boot, beginning with the letter, P, did David first endorse with the company Adidas?

15 Did Fenerbahce, Real Madrid or Juventus break Manchester United's long running unbeaten home record in European games?

16 How many Premiership games did each team play in the 1999-2000 season?

17 He bought Victoria a £50,000 black diamond ring on what occasion?

18 Which young Manchester United player followed Steve McClaren to Middlesbrough?

19 How many goals did David score for Preston North End whilst on loan?

20 What is the title of Victoria's book about her life?

21 What part of his body did David injure during the last ever England game at Wembley?

22 Which of the following players did not take part in the 2001 Pepsi Challenge: Rui Costa, Dwight Yorke, Roberto Carlos, Rivaldo, Kieron Dyer, David Beckham, Les Ferdinand?

23 In what year did Manchester United win the Intercontinental Cup?

24 In which country did he and Victoria get married?

25 In what position did Manchester United finish in the last season of Division One before it became the Premiership?

WORDSEARCH 3

```
N J N E V I L L E D D A
B A W P N L K Q N K K B
L B L W H C W A E T R R
A F D R T M N L D O W E
N U S G O I A C W H F A
C L N I D F E N D B T J
K P L R L N R Z V U B K
I S E O U V O B U T B S
G F E T R X E E K T A L
E I R L O R K S O F R O
Y O G W O E A C T J T S
F L W G A H B C P R H X
O Z Y N S I C T V T E M
P K E I E V X S H R Z C
```

Barthez	Ferdinand	Neville
Blanc	Forlan	Scholes
Brown	Fortune	Silvestre
Butt	Giggs	Solskjaer
Carroll	Keane	

(See answers on p152.)

1. Who was the goalkeeper David beat with a 57 yard shot in 1996?

2. Which newspaper printed a dartboard with his face as the bull's-eye following his sending off in the 1998 World Cup?

3. In what year did he score his fiftieth goal for Manchester United?

4. GQ magazine awarded David what "best" title?

5. In what year did the Spice Girls become a four person group?

6. A painting showing David as the mythical god, Jupiter, was auctioned over the Internet but for which British children's charity?

7. Against which English team did he score his first goal at Wembley?

8. At which ground, no longer around, did he make his debut for the full Manchester United team?

9   Beckham's first major football boot sponsorship deal was with Reebok, Adidas or Nike?

10 Before they were the Spice Girls, the band were known as: The Point, Touch, The Queen Bees or Attraction?

11 In the 2001 Pepsi Challenge football skills contest, in what place did David finish?

12 In 1987, David was a mascot for Manchester United when they played against which team?

13 What was the name of the little girl that David held hands with at the 2002 Commonwealth Games opening ceremony?

14 *City Life* magazine voted David the Mancunian of the Year but in which year?

15 The Watford professional footballer, Micah Hyde, played with David in which junior team?

16 *Company* magazine voted David Beckham the world's sexiest man in 2002. Which pop singer did he knock off the top spot?

17 Which player took David's previous shirt number seeing him switch to number seven?

18 Whilst at Preston, David scored a goal against a team who are now in the Premiership. Can you name the team?

19 Is the number tattooed on David written in Hindi, in English or as Roman numerals?

20 Against which Israeli team did Manchester United suffer a surprise away defeat in the 2002-2003 Champions League?

21 Which Manchester United player was sent off in the second Manchester derby match of the 2001-2002 season?

22 After 34 international games, how many goals had David scored for England?

23 Which football manager offered to sell his car number plate "POSH" to Victoria?

24 Who did Manchester United beat to win the Intercontinental Cup in 1999?

25 What European competition had Manchester United won several months before David signed as a youth trainee?

Turn over the page for the final Penalty Shootout ...

Play against a friend, taking turns to read out and answer the questions. If the scores are level after five questions each, whoever gets closest to the sudden death question is the winner.

(See answers on p145.)

Penalty Shootout 5

A1 Which South American team, beginning with the letter P, did England play in a friendly in 2002?

B1 David came on as a substitute in an England friendly held at Old Trafford in 1997. Against which African team was the game?

A2 Which Portuguese team did Manchester United beat 4-0 in the 1996-1997 season?

B2 From which country was the team that broke Manchester United's unbeaten home record in Europe?

A3 In 1994, was David part of a champion-ship-winning first team, reserve team or youth team at Manchester United?

B3 In 1999 David was voted Best Midfielder by the Premiership, UEFA or FIFA?

A4 In March 2002, Manchester United played a great 5-3 victory over which team?

B4 Against which Premiership team did Manchester United score six goals in the 2001-2002 season?

A5 In his dream team for Rage, did David choose Fabien Barthez, Peter Schmeichel or Mark Bosnich as goalkeeper?

B5 In his dream team, did David choose Andy Cole, Mark Hughes or Ruud van Nistelrooy in the number nine position?

Sudden Death Question

In what year did Manchester United finish with their lowest ever league points total?

ANSWERS

WARM UPS 1

1. England
2. Married
3. Manchester United
4. False
5. Seven
6. British
7. The Spice Girls
8. False
9. True
10. Yes
11. Victoria
12. Posh Spice
13. False
14. Argentina
15. 1998
16. Gary and Phil Neville
17. Seven
18. True
19. Third
20. A part of New York
21. Ryan Giggs
22. A sarong
23. His father
24. True
25. Arsenal

WARM UPS 2

1. Wayne Rooney
2. One
3. True
4. False
5. Yes
6. Brooklyn
7. Japan
8. Sir Alex Ferguson
9. London
10. False
11. Yes
12. David Beckham
13. Juan Veron
14. False
15. Marks and Spencers
16. Brazil
17. True
18. Thrones
19. His toe
20. True
21. 2002
22. Too small
23. True
24. Manchester United and Manchester City
25. Son

WARM UPS 3

1. Scotland
2. Midfield
3. Gary
4. Free
5. True
6. Half an eyebrow
7. Tony Blair
8. An indoor pool
9. True
10. Sweden
11. Dwight Yorke and Andy Cole
12. True
13. The FA Cup
14. False
15. More than 60,000
16. False
17. Coventry
18. Two
19. Almost always
20. True
21. David Beckham
22. Last
23. Holland
24. False
25. True

 # FIRST HALF
Question rating: MEDIUM

FIRST HALF 1

1. 16 goals
2. True
3. Caroline
4. Colombia
5. A basketball player
6. Alan Shearer
7. 9,000
8. La Manga
9. Villa Park
10. True
11. Europe
12. Gianfranco Zola
13. True
14. Four
15. Victoria & Albert Museum
16. Romania
17. His sister (Joanne)
18. Diego Forlan
19. Bognor Regis
20. Deepdale
21. 13
22. Sir Alex Ferguson
23. Japan
24. Joseph
25. True

FIRST HALF 2

1. Eric Cantona
2. Liverpool
3. True
4. Roses
5. True
6. Venice
7. Roy Keane
8. Once
9. *Bend It Like Beckham*
10. FIFA World Club Championship
11. Jade Jagger
12. Sir Bobby Charlton
13. Juan Veron
14. Bishop of Cork
15. Tunisia
16. Channel 5
17. Manchester
18. Chelsea
19. 1989
20. Glenn Hoddle
21. False
22. Colombia
23. Yes
24. Ten
25. Teddy Sheringham

FIRST HALF 3

1. 100 metres
2. Third
3. True

4. *Match of the Day*
5. Five
6. Purple
7. The Busby Babes
8. His name was spelt wrongly on his shirt
9. Seven
10. An angel
11. Borussia Dortmund
12. Sir Alex Ferguson
13. South-east Asia
14. Mike Tyson
15. Poland
16. Ryan Giggs
17. Manchester United
18. 57 goals
19. Chelsea
20. 97.9 mph
21. Calf
22. Brooklyn
23. True
24. Ron Atkinson
25. Argentina

FIRST HALF 4

1. South Africa
2. Moldova
3. Second seeds
4. All of those things
5. Came second
6. Italy
7. France

8. Playing golf
9. Eric Cantona
10. Himself
11. Prince Charles
12. Sven-Goran Eriksson
13. Where he played his first proper matches
14. Liverpool
15. Manchester United
16. "Fergie's Fledglings"
17. 16
18. Greece
19. Chelsea
20. True
21. Victoria
22. Bryan Robson
23. The Manchester United scout who signed David
24. True
25. Romeo

FIRST HALF 5

1. David's dad
2. Four (40 years)
3. Fenerbahce
4. West Bromwich Albion
5. Waltham Forest
6. Old Trafford
7. David's mother

8. Two
9. A two or three step run-up
10. Her knickers
11. Australia
12. 1996
13. Georgia
14. Paul Scholes
15. Michael Owen
16. The creator of David's first tattoo
17. Gary Neville
18. 2-2
19. 1997
20. False
21. Italy
22. First
23. False
24. Kosovo
25. The Premier League and the FA Cup

FIRST HALF 6

1. LKS Lodz
2. Aston Villa
3. Tommy Docherty
4. True
5. 1930s
6. Free kick
7. True
8. Yes
9. Le Tournoi
10. Blackburn Rovers

11. Laurent Blanc
12. Geri Halliwell
13. 43
14. Chelsea
15. True
16. New York
17. Never
18. Quarter-finals
19. Computer games
20. England Under 21 team
21. Sophie Ellis-Bextor
22. Once
23. Spain
24. False
25. True

FIRST HALF 7

1. Bayern Munich
2. Bradford (Valley Parade) and Charlton (The Valley)
3. Newcastle United
4. 'Wannabe'
5. Jordi Cruyff
6. Barcelona
7. July
8. Ali G
9. True
10. Yes
11. Brondby
12. Wembley
13. 2-2

14. West Bromwich Albion
15. Newspaper advert
16. Tony Adams
17. A blue Porsche
18. Champions League
19. Italy
20. David Beckham
21. 7-0
22. Group D
23. Fourteen
24. Moody Productions
25. Blackburn Rovers

FIRST HALF 8

1. Over twelve million pounds
2. Bayern Munich
3. Jaap Stam
4. Keith Gillespie
5. Bury
6. First
7. Younger
8. Italy
9. Arsenal
10. Japanese
11. Turkey
12. Paul Scholes
13. Liverpool
14. FA Youth Cup
15. Colombia
16. They were getting married

17. *Spiceworld*
18. Rap
19. Eleven
20. Spurs
21. Birthday emails
22. South Korea and Japan
23. Preston North End
24. True
25. France

FIRST HALF 9

1. His boots
2. Organised a trial with Manchester United
3. 1998-1999
4. Concorde
5. Centre of midfield
6. Paul Ince
7. £1,600
8. Kevin Keegan
9. Gary Lineker
10. True
11. Macedonia
12. NSPCC
13. Manchester United 4 Newcastle United 3
14. Eight
15. All eight
16. 1992
17. Barcelona
18. Victoria

19. Owen Hargreaves
20. One day
21. Paul Gascoigne
22. Juan Sebastian Veron
23. Hertfordshire
24. Belgium and Holland
25. Michael Jordan

FIRST HALF 10

1. Netball
2. Got engaged
3. Goldenballs
4. Mick Jagger
5. Second
6. Luis Figo
7. Spurs
8. France
9. True
10. 1-1 draw
11. Fulham
12. True
13. France
14. Sweden
15. Juan Veron
16. Leeds United
17. Romania
18. Ryan Giggs
19. Liverpool
20. £50,000
21. Portugal
22. Five
23. Manchester City

24. A defeat
25. Eric Cantona

FIRST HALF 11

1. Michael Owen
2. True
3. Eric Cantona
4. Roy Keane
5. True
6. Kevin Keegan
7. Spain
8. Alan Hansen
9. Peter Schmeichel
10. After his sending off in the 1998 World Cup
11. 25 years
12. None
13. The mohican
14. Mexico
15. Mark Hughes
16. False
17. True
18. The opera
19. 1997
20. 'Three Lions'
21. Kevin Keegan
22. More than 50
23. Given a yellow card
24. True
25. Bolton Wanderers

 SECOND HALF
Question rating: MEDIUM

SECOND HALF 1

1. September
2. Pink
3. Pride Park (Derby)
4. Spurs
5. Gary Neville's
6. David's mother
7. Second half
8. A gas engineer
9. Mark Hughes
10. 2002 World Cup
11. Sent off
12. Germany
13. Arm
14. Every game
15. Division Three
16. Smallest
17. True
18. A sarong
19. Finland
20. Howard Wilkinson
21. Anfield
22. 2000

23. Came second
24. Four
25. False

SECOND HALF 2

1. Three seasons
2. Arsenal
3. Champions League
4. Germany
5. Win
6. Villa Park
7. Muhammad Ali
8. Newcastle United
9. Leeds United
10. Jewish
11. Five
12. A draw
13. *Only Fools and Horses*
14. Manchester United
15. Toe
16. FA Youth Cup
17. Two dogs
18. Lazio
19. Wembley Stadium
20. Teddy Sheringham
21. Geri Halliwell
22. Nantes
23. Brooklyn
24. Shinpads
25. A Ford Escort

SECOND HALF 3

1. Peter Taylor
2. Preston North End
3. Bodyguard
4. Old Trafford
5. Beckingham Palace
6. *Tank Girl*
7. His father
8. Denmark (3-0)
9. Free kick
10. Tottenham Hotspur
11. Clothing range
12. Victoria's
13. 1996
14. Austria
15. Rottweilers
16. True
17. Leeds United
18. BMW Series 5
19. Eric Cantona
20. Holly Valance and Nicole Appleton
21. Andy Hinchcliffe
22. Sweden
23. Leytonstone
24. Seven
25. True

SECOND HALF 4

1. Lazio
2. *The Beano*

3. Argentina
4. 1999
5. Victoria's parents'
6. Ash and Atomic Kitten
7. Greece
8. Van Nistelrooy or Solksjaer
9. Juan Veron
10. Victoria's publicity agent
11. True
12. None
13. Stevie Wonder
14. Spanish
15. Before
16. Five
17. Golf
18. Carrington
19. 1999
20. Graham Taylor
21. True
22. Victoria
23. 2000
24. MUTV
25. A hairdresser

SECOND HALF 5

1. Sir Bobby Charlton
2. 1999
3. Diego Simeone
4. Two sisters
5. 1998
6. The Premiership

7. Gary Lineker
8. Another boy took food from the kitchen
9. 2001
10. Argentinean
11. Persuasion
12. Tottenham Hotspur
13. The Queen
14. Bryan Robson
15. Ridgeway Rovers
16. True
17. 1991
18. Manchester United
19. Theatre of Dreams
20. Thailand
21. None
22. True
23. Laine Arts Theatre School
24. 25
25. 6,000

SECOND HALF 6

1. Alderley Edge
2. True
3. David and Victoria's wedding
4. True
5. Dwight Yorke
6. A number two shaved cut
7. False

8. True
9. Sir Alex Ferguson
10. Brighton and Hove Albion
11. *David Beckham: My World*
12. Ridgeway Rovers
13. 101 goals
14. His son, Brooklyn
15. LA Lakers
16. Bayern Munich
17. Fabien Barthez
18. Gary Neville
19. 16 goals
20. Howard Wilkinson
21. Volkswagen Golf
22. Leyton Orient
23. Aberdeen
24. Hair stylist
25. Swimming pool

SECOND HALF 7

1. Wimbledon
2. Eric Cantona
3. England Under 21
4. 1992
5. False
6. *Bend It Like Beckham*
7. Steve Bruce
8. Denmark
9. Chinese
10. True
11. Both ears

12. Victoria's ex-boyfriend
13. A basketball game
14. 2001
15. Rumbelows Cup
16. A referee who sent David off
17. Brylcreem
18. One
19. True
20. Glenn Hoddle
21. Chairman
22. 1998-1999
23. Newcastle United
24. Manchester City
25. Ribs

SECOND HALF 8

1. True
2. Germany 1 England 5
3. Sir Bobby Charlton
4. Robbie Fowler
5. Very neat and tidy
6. Nottingham
7. Southampton
8. Once
9. Pepsi
10. Peterborough United
11. Slovakia
12. Teddy Sheringham
13. 2002
14. Greece

15. Green
16. Kevin Keegan
17. QPR
18. Rap artists
19. David Beckham
20. Deportivo La Coruna
21. Sunday mornings
22. Albania
23. 'Hey Diddle Diddle'
24. Uruguay
25. Steve McClaren

13. A Rolls Royce
14. Once
15. True
16. Glenn Hoddle
17. His grandfather
18. *OK* magazine
19. True
20. Gary Neville
21. Manchester United
22. His dad
23. A month
24. Romania
25. London

SECOND HALF 9

1. Cucumber sushi
2. Umbro
3. Tottenham Hotspur
4. Middle
5. Released as a single in 2000
6. 180cm
7. The Commonwealth Games
8. Terry Venables
9. Nottingham Forest
10. Between one and two thousand pounds
11. Japan
12. Deportivo La Coruna

SECOND HALF 10

1. Manchester United's reserves
2. False
3. A car
4. Lazio
5. Los Angeles
6. 1986
7. Terry Venables
8. Applaud
9. True
10. Essex
11. Roy Keane
12. Comic Relief
13. Scotland
14. Peter Schmeichel
15. Champions League
16. Sol Campbell
17. Manchester City

18. The first newspaper photo
19. They got an injury after using all their substitutes
20. Southampton
21. Sir Alex Ferguson
22. Basle
23. Five
24. Italy
25. Six

SECOND HALF 11

1. Juventus
2. 13
3. Hindi
4. Spain
5. Juan Veron
6. David James
7. A record of Victoria's

8. Spurs
9. Rio Ferdinand
10. 1991
11. Four – Blanc, Barthez, Butt and Brown
12. Ruud Van Nistelrooy
13. Gary Neville
14. Complaining about the food
15. James
16. Czech Republic
17. Uri Geller
18. Nicky Butt
19. Most caring
20. Belgium
21. 1909
22. Manchester United
23. Birmingham
24. Blackburn Rovers
25. Andrei Kanchelskis

 TOUGH TO TACKLE
Question rating: HARD

TOUGH TO TACKLE 1

1. Selby Town
2. One (David Beckham)
3. Upton Park
4. Ten pounds
5. Ridgeway Rovers

6. Paul Scholes
7. Jordi Cruyff
8. Ridgeway Rovers
9. Little Devil
10. 101
11. Holland
12. Three

13. 'Out of Your Mind'
14. Leicester City
15. October
16. Phil Neville
17. Darren Anderton
18. Sturm Graz
19. West Ham
20. Six
21. Aston Villa
22. Gary Neville, Nicky Butt, Paul Scholes
23. 1974
24. Poland
25. 2001-2002 season

TOUGH TO TACKLE 2

1. 14 years old
2. Anderlecht
3. A Jaffa Cake
4. Crystal Palace
5. Leeds United and Lincoln City
6. David Batty
7. Brazil
8. One
9. Seventeen
10. Nobby Stiles
11. David's equalising goal against Greece
12. The United States
13. Bayer Leverkusen (Hans-Jorg Butt)
14. Nicky Butt

15. 24
16. 42
17. Solskjaer
18. Eight
19. Barcelona
20. Ryan Giggs
21. Selhurst Park
22. Blackburn Rovers
23. He made his England debut
24. Gun bullets
25. Paul Ince

TOUGH TO TACKLE 3

1. Five
2. He became a father
3. Second Division
4. A Ford Escort
5. Paul Scholes
6. 1966-1967 season
7. Tom Wood
8. Brian McClair
9. Sir Alex Ferguson
10. 1997
11. 1500 metres
12. 1999-2000
13. Seven
14. His father
15. Eleven
16. 'Say You'll Be There'
17. Leeds United
18. United States

19. Brazil
20. Elton John's
21. 1992-1993
22. 1999-2000
23. Seven
24. 1974
25. Liverpool

TOUGH TO TACKLE 4

1. *Beauty and the Beast*
2. Chelsea
3. 5-0 to Chelsea
4. A greyhound track
5. 11
6. Wrexham
7. Phil Neville
8. Luke Chadwick
9. Honda Prelude
10. Edgar Davids
11. Nottingham Forest
12. The Cliff
13. Speeding in his car
14. Predator
15. Fenerbahce
16. 38
17. Their first wedding anniversary
18. Jonathon Greening
19. Two
20. *Learning To Fly*
21. His knee
22. Kieron Dyer, Les Ferdinand

23. 1999
24. Ireland
25. Second

TOUGH TO TACKLE 5

1. Neil Sullivan
2. The *Daily Mirror*
3. 2000
4. Best-dressed man
5. 1998
6. NSPCC
7. Newcastle United
8. Goldstone Ground
9. Adidas
10. Touch
11. Third
12. West Ham
13. Kirsty Howard
14. 2001
15. Ridgeway Rovers
16. Robbie Williams
17. Teddy Sheringham
18. Fulham
19. Roman numerals
20. Maccabi Haifa
21. Roy Keane
22. One
23. Barry Fry
24. Palmeiras
25. The European Cup Winners Cup

PENALTY SHOOTOUT 1

A1. False
B1. True
A2. Maine Road
B2. Manchester City 3
   Manchester United 1
A3. "Choccy"
B3. 90 appearances
A4. Artificial legs
B4. Team chef
A5. Leeds United
B5. Liverpool
Sudden Death: 1106 Points

PENALTY SHOOTOUT 2

A1. Portugal
B1. Brazil
A2. Every four years
B2. Every four years
A3. FA Cup
B3. Mark Bosnich
A4. Portugal
B4. Leicester City
A5. Cameroon
B5. Malta
Sudden Death: 103

PENALTY SHOOTOUT 3

A1. Kevin Keegan
B1. Luxembourg
A2. Nine

B2. 15
A3. 1997
B3. 43
A4. Bolton Wanderers
B4. Both
A5. Eleven
B5. Tottenham Hotspur
Sudden Death: 246

PENALTY SHOOTOUT 4

A1. First
B1. Gary Neville
A2. Dion Dublin
B2. Paul Ince
A3. Everton
B3. Penguins
A4. Victoria
B4. Sol Campbell
A5. Aries
B5. Taurus
Sudden Death: Fourteen

PENALTY SHOOTOUT 5

A1. Paraguay
B1. South Africa
A2. FC Porto
B2. Turkey
A3. Reserve team
B3. UEFA
A4. West Ham
B4. Southampton

A5. Fabien Barthez   Sudden Death: 1894

B5. Mark Hughes   (14 points)

MATCH FIT 1

St James Park	Newcastle United
White Hart Lane	Tottenham Hotspur
Riverside	Middlesbrough
The Valley	Charlton Athletic
Goodison Park	Everton
St Andrews	Birmingham City
The Stadium of Light	Sunderland
The Reebok Stadium	Bolton Wanderers
St Mary's Stadium	Southampton
Maine Road	Manchester City

MATCH FIT 2

The Gunners	Arsenal
The Owls	Sheffield Wednesday
The Canaries	Norwich
The Toffees	Everton
The Saints	Southampton
The Black Cats	Sunderland
The Hammers	West Ham United
The Baggies	West Bromwich Albion
The Foxes	Leicester City
The Rams	Derby County

MATCH FIT 3

Peter Reid	Sunderland
Arsene Wenger	Arsenal
Sam Allardyce	Bolton Wanderers
Gordon Strachan	Southampton
Sir Bobby Robson	Newcastle United
David Moyes	Everton
Gary Megson	West Bromwich Albion
Graham Taylor	Aston Villa
Gerard Houllier	Liverpool
Glen Roeder	West Ham

MATCH FIT 4

Barcelona	Spain
Bayern Munich	Germany
FC Basle	Switzerland
PSV Eindhoven	Holland
Paris St. Germain	France
Rosenborg	Norway
Dinamo Zagreb	Croatia
Deportivo La Coruna	Spain
Parma	Italy
IFK Gothenburg	Sweden

MATCH FIT 5

Barcelona	Nou Camp
Internazionale	San Siro
Bayer Leverkusen	BayArena
Olympiakos	Lefkosia
Galatasaray	Ali Semi Yen
Fiorentina	Artemio Franchi
Real Madrid	Bernabeu
Dynamo Kiev	Olympic Stadium
Anderlecht	Constant Vanden Stock
Marseilles	Velodrome Stadium

CROSSING PUZZLE 1

H   AT-TRICK
O   WEN
D   ROP BALL
D   RIBBLING
L   ESLEY
E   LEVEN

CROSSING PUZZLE 3

R   ONALDO
O   LDHAM
B   USBY
S   CHOLES
O   BSTRUCTION
N   EWCASTLE UNITED

CROSSING PUZZLE 2

V   IDUKA
I   PSWICH
C   ROSS
T   HROW-IN
O   WN GOAL
R   EDKNAPP
I   NDIRECT
A   THLETIC

ANAGRAMS 1

Barthez
Neville
Forlan
Fortune
Scholes
Carroll

ANAGRAMS 2

Seaman
Gerrard
Bridge
Fowler
Heskey
Vassell

ANAGRAMS 3

Hughes
Cruyff
Cantona
Johnsen
Bosnich
Dublin

ANAGRAMS 4

Sweden
Denmark
Albania
Ukraine
Finland
Mexico

WORDSEARCH 1

WORDSEARCH 2

```
D  P  I  E  N  E  D  E  W  S  T  S
U  O  D  T  J  O  C  I  X  E  M  O
U  L  W  X  R  P  E  N  J  G  I  H
Y  A  N  I  T  N  E  G  R  A  O  O
A  N  D  P  I  F  D  Y  Y  L  P  L
H  D  G  A  O  Y  N  W  L  O  U  I
Q  F  R  J  G  A  L  A  X  U  P  Z
M  K  F  R  M  R  N  A  I  O  I  A
U  V  B  R  V  D  E  L  T  Y  P  R
J  J  E  B  A  V  S  E  J  I  Y  B
B  G  A  I  N  O  D  E  C  A  M  X
A  L  B  A  N  I  A  I  B  E  T  R
L  C  X  X  C  O  L  O  M  B  I  A
L  X  A  V  O  D  L  O  M  V  C  S
```

WORDSEARCH 3